Fulfilment Now

Celebrating Life

Extracted from the Teachings of

Shaykh Fadhlalla Haeri

Zahra Publications

Published by Zahra Publications
Centurion
South Africa

E-mail: info@shaykhfadhlallahaeri.com
info@sfhfoundation.net
© 2022 Shaykh Fadhlalla Haeri

All Rights Reserved.
Except for brief quotations in critical articles or reviews,
no part of this book may be reproduced or utilised
in any form or by any means,
electronic or mechanical, without permission in writing
from the publisher.

Designed and typeset in South Africa by
Mizpah Marketing Concepts

To purchase an eBook version of this book
kindly visit www.zahrapublications.pub

For further information on Shaykh Fadhlalla Haeri and
his teaching please visit www.shaykhfadhlallahaeri.com

The photograph of Shaykh Haeri on pg 133 was taken by AbuBakr Karolia

ISBN: 978-1-928329-34-3

Table of Contents

	Acknowledgements	5
	Introduction	9
1.	Origins	11
2.	Life's Purpose	19
3.	Self and Soul	27
4.	The Rise to Higher Consciousness	35
5.	The Perpetual Now	41
6.	The Driving Forces in Life	47
7.	Certainty and Uncertainty	63
8.	The Teacher and the Seeker	69
9.	Levels of Consciousness	77
10.	The Question of Free Will	83
11.	Personal Will and Destiny	89
12.	Presence	97
13.	Death and Eternal Life	101
14.	Service, Identity and Belonging	109
15.	Relationships	115
16.	Justice	121
17.	A Fulfilled Life	127
	Postscript	132

Shaykh Fadhlalla Haeri

Acknowledgements

This book arose out of a question posed to Shaykh Fadhlalla Haeri about what it is like to live a fulfilled life. Thanks to Aliya B. Haeri for initiating and seeing the project of this book through to its completion and to Abbas Bilgrami for the invaluable production advice and design. Acknowledgment is also due to three key contributors of time and skills: Mohamed Bulbulia, Hasnayn Ebrahim and Muna H. Bilgrami.

The Tulip Motif

The tulip motif used throughout this book is from a Turkish Iznik design, and represents perfect, deep love. Originally from the Persian, the word for tulip, laleh, possesses orthographic and onomatopoeic similarities to the word Allah. As such the tulip symbolizes the object of spiritual meditation, and simultaneously represents humility for when it is in full bloom, it bows its head before the majesty of God. The tulip motif appears in this book as a recurring symbol of meditation and fulfilment of perfect love through humbling oneself in the presence of God.

Cover Painting

The painting used as the cover artwork for Fulfilment Now is by Shaykh Fadhlalla Haeri. He was inspired to produce this stunning oil colour as part of a series that he drew in a span of three weeks.

'Our experience on earth is based on movement and change within space and time. Whatever begins or starts will end. So will all the great planets, stars, and galaxies. As for the meaning and purpose of this life on earth, it is to prepare us for a much higher level of consciousness, not conditioned as we are within our embodiment on earth.'
Shaykh Fadhlalla Haeri

Introduction

Fulfilment is the act or process of achievement of something desired, promised, or predicted.

You are alive now. The past may have left some traces. As for the future, it holds hope and uncertainties. What is sure is now, the instant. The flickering, moving sense of time which has emerged from the Unseen, leads to the future, and leaves a trace in the past. It has emerged from timelessness and eternal truth.

The human soul is our link to eternal life and leads us to a natural drive to rising consciousness due to the agency of intelligence. We desire contentment, ease, and effortless flow along the path of our destiny. Any living entity emerges from the source of life to experience all possible variations and then subsides back to life's source itself.

Intelligent living creatures seek goodness and fulfilment in the present moment, as well as hope for the future to also provide that joyful presence. We seek and aspire to what is constant and eternal and that is the nature of the divine spirit within the heart, ever perfect, timeless, and eternal.

This book views "a fulfilled life" as a life where our being emerges from higher, or supreme, consciousness. The calibration between our conditioned consciousness and higher consciousness reduces suffering. A fulfilled life means we realise that this life is a transitory, temporary stage between the finite known and the infinite unknown, or between the self and the soul.

The way to true fulfilment is through self-realisation and ultimately being at one with eternal Oneness.

Chapter One

Origins

What is the Origin of the Universe?

How did it begin?

Origin of the Universe

Questions about the beginnings and the endings of the universe, or universes; our individual beginnings and potential demise; our role in the cosmos and the resultant meaning and purpose of life with all its challenges and joys – these questions are frequently asked by people of intellect.

As far as we can ascertain, the origin of our universe – and the many which may exist parallel to it – lies in a single, infinitely dense point which began expanding 14 billion years ago and has continued to do so up to the present moment. A few thousand years ago, reflective thinkers and prophets provided the idea that there is one Supreme God that encompasses all that is known and unknown and that this creation occurred as a mysterious event due to God's will.

Some three and a half billion years ago, emergent from God's 'mind', or Supreme Consciousness, was a consciousness of a major attribute, one we describe as 'eternal-living', which sparked the advent of life. With it came the memory and recognition of Life itself and it was primarily focused on preservation. As it occurred, this spark caused life to become obsessed with Life and with it the requirement for it to connect with physical universality. It had to be the semipermeable membrane: give and take. It was not fixed and insulated for it had to connect with the 'outside'. As time went by, this led to the evolution of consciousness towards awareness of consciousness. This inevitability was due to the recognition of its source and the reality that all there is, is the light of God.

A few hundred thousand years ago consciousness of consciousness took root, as captured in the story of Adam. Revealed knowledge depicts Adam as the shadow or steward of God on earth because of his capacity for higher consciousness. This is reflected in our lives today: our consciousness and the understanding of the ant preserving its life and the wasp defending itself. This is a celebration of life: the sting of the wasp is its defence *and* the preservation of life. The obsession with Life is the most potent natural drive towards the source of life which is eternal and boundless.

How did it all begin?

An untold number of different lights, beams, flavours, colours, stages and states of intensity all emerged from, and will return to, its Origin, Supreme Consciousness. This all occurred in no time. In our present context we would say this occurred over a few billion years; yet, it all emerged from non-time! We must then question what difference does it make whether it was sixteen billion or five billion, or no time at all?

What can be said is that it all emerged from One cosmic source in a fraction of a second. The billions of stars and galaxies and all that we observe around us in the sky emerged from the unknown and is expanding, due to so-called 'dark' or hidden energy.

Matter emerged from cosmic energy and began to coalesce into the elements and physical entities with which we are familiar. Primordial reality contained everything within it but not in a discernible way that would fit into descriptions like solid or liquid, hot or cold. It is from this unseen reality that what is visible emerged. From the absolute potential of everything, or nonexistence, every imaginable manifestation has emerged.

Two Zones of Consciousness

There are two zones of consciousness. One is discernible, leaving traces on the mind and memory, open to interpretation and discussion. This zone of consciousness, which we call conditioned consciousness, can be changed and corroborated. We can say: 'Yes, we know this event happened, and we saw this stone falling.' This is the world of physical, chemical, visible realities in which we can all share. It is a temporary reality and it has definable qualities.

The Absolute zone is a cosmic, boundless, and timeless zone which is permanent, perpetual, and constant. The cosmic source is not confined or conditioned by space or time, and it is where we assume divinity resides. Another way of describing these two zones is as the absolute and the relative zones of consciousness. Anything that appears on earth has both a touch of the infinite as well as characteristics of the finite.

Self-Reflection Questions:

1. How would you maintain being in the absolute zone of consciousness whilst simultaneously engaging in your conditioned life?

Chapter Two

Life's Purpose

Who am I?

What is the purpose of my life?

Who am I?

The foundation of our physical reality is light – the photon. It behaves as a particle when observed, with a unique identity and specific position in space and time. Yet, the photon also behaves as a wave, describing a probability amplitude when no observer is present, which is the potential of light itself spread across all space and time.

As a particle, it has a beginning and an end, with measurable effects and duration. As a wave, it is continuous everywhere, always. In truth it is neither particle nor wave and is therefore a potent metaphor for existence itself. Its origin is celestial, but it manifests in the terrestrial. It is from the absolute but appears as, and in, the relative world.

The same applies to every human. The soul has all the qualities of timelessness, but it appears with a birth and a death, beginning and an end. It is a universal entity transiting through a local state. The universal energy that appears has certain differentiable qualities such as species, size, colour, and other characteristics of living entities.

Unconditionality is pure potential that is not bound, constrained or discernible. Anything that appears or manifests, be it solid, liquid or anything else for that matter, becomes an experience and is confined to space and time. It is the extent of space and time which modulates that conditionality. This may be for millions of years, or it may be for a second.

The human being is a clear mix between a pure infinite energy source and its conditioned earthly, material, physical, chemical, and biological characteristics. Everything has emerged from the infinite unseen and returns to it. This is our ultimate destiny.

What is the purpose of my life?

We cannot function or experience anything in this life unless it is mediated by our minds, which connects the visible, sensory, material, and discernible with the source of energy that is the spirit or soul. The mind is between our spirit and soul, our so-called human being. You and I, we are between humanity and divinity, and the mind is the meeting point on which both hinge. That is why we say, 'He is unhinged,' if the mind is not functional. You need the mind to function in the material, physical, chemical, and emotional zone of experience.

We are here to experience all of this and then to give it back, retaining only a few traces after we leave the body and the mind. These traces are carried after death and can be imagined as the soul's fingerprint. Even these traces must be returned if we are to return fully to Oneness, which is the meaning of purgatory or hell and paradise. These words refer to a zone in which the traces we carry are either burnt off or washed gently away.

If I had serious desires and curbed them, or I was responsible and reverent, I may get what I missed or desired in this life instantly after death in the unseen. I may be liberated from my lust, desires and so on. Equally, if I have interfered with nature, or committed crimes, so too must I be rid of these things. They will burn off.

The purpose of this life is to be prepared for the next life where we can no longer act and change our minds or emotions. We are helpless in that zone. We will experience the next life according to how well we have prepared and groomed ourselves during this phase, which is the inverse of what is to come.

In this life, the material, physical, and chemical prevail. Identity and personality prevail over the energy source or the source of life in us. After death, it is the reverse. What appears is life itself, with only a shadow or trace of the so-called person. Here, I first see the person, the shadow, the material, the flesh and the bone, the colour of the skin; only later do I see they are also a soul. After death you first see the light that is giving the shadow its temporary reality.

Thus, we can be best described as stewards in this life. We function as though we are in charge. For instance, I am in control of my body and what I do, what I think, how much I eat, and how I rest. I am a steward of my body and mind. However, I am only an apprentice. If I do well, then my entry into the next life is easy. That is why the religious injunctions or teachings prepare us to enter the next life without a great deal of pain and suffering. The degree to which we take care of ourselves and exercise our stewardship is under constant review. This is a major thing. I am here in training, as an apprentice, so that I become aware of every moment and its eternal connectedness with whatever occurs right now.

Self-Reflection Questions:

1. You are an infinite being traveling through time and space as a finite self. Reflect on how this influences the kind of life you want to lead.

    - What one thing can you do today that will facilitate living the life you want?

Chapter Three

Self and Soul

What is the nature and characteristics of the self and the soul?

What does it mean to align self and soul?

Nature of the Self and Soul

Reality, truth or the divine power is that constant from which all other temporary emergences take place. The human soul carries the imprint of eternal Divine Reality. It is the source of human life and consciousness. Our earthly experience is based on consciousness of dualities and, as such, the soul provides a shadow of itself, which is the ego-self.

Nothing is experienced in this world unless it is in pairs, dualities, pluralities, or multiplicities. Every sentient entity has two aspects. One is heavenly, celestial, unseen energy and the other is earthly, terrestrial, visible and discernible, with chemical, physical and material characteristics. Every one of us and every moment contains two aspects: one emanates as pure energy from the zone of the absolute, the other appears as transient, relative, and changing.

The first can be considered a quantum field of possibilities, continuous throughout space and time. The other is a physical reality which is discernible and measurable. The nature of anything once discerned is specific rather than a spectrum. For example, consider a child on a sports field. Though they may be able to visualise themselves doing any number of things, they are limited by their desire to be seen by their parents. The desire to be seen narrows the continuous spectrum into a discernible action. The two zones are in constant interchange and are inseparable, though observation makes the connection seem uncertain.

I, you, he, she and every one of us have a soul or spirit, which is a plug that connects us with life itself. People refer to truth as reality, absolute, or God. You can equally call it Cosmic Life. Wherever you look, you will find this Life, though it does not manifest. The nearest example we can understand is that of fire. The essence of fire, or the soul of fire, is everywhere but it does not manifest until the conditions required to connect the essence of fire with visible flame are met. These conditions are a spark and fuel that the spark can ignite, and which will give the flame temporary life. To maintain its appearance of ongoing-ness and the connection between essence and visibility, the flame must be fed with more material.

The essence of the fire was there before, as with the soul of human beings or anything alive. They were there in the unseen, but they did not manifest until the right conditions in the womb or egg were met and the soul or spirit descended from the unseen. Just as with fire and flame, it is always there, but may not be discernible, measurable, or visible. Like a flame, the foetus must be fed for it to maintain an earthly appearance of ongoing-ness, which is a property of the soul within.

Whatever appears on earth is dependent on the total, invisible Absoluteness. The Absolute is not dependent. It is pure energy, greater than any level of consciousness. Once it becomes conscious of something, it then becomes dependent on a set of conditions being met to maintain its life. Life is always there, but once it becomes 'me' I must become concerned about maintaining it. Quite naturally, I am obsessed with life because it is the biggest gift Supreme Consciousness can bestow. Whatever I do has as its foundation this first loyalty, duty, love, and obsession with life itself.

When life appeared from the composition of basic elements with certain physical and chemical characteristics, its first concern was to take care of itself. Life is aware of life. It points toward ongoingness and perpetuity. Everything that exists has a connection, as it has emerged from a zone of continuous, perpetual connectedness, so it has a trace of that memory. It wants to continue. Anything that is tasted, touched, or experienced in life wants to continue living. This is the first and primary objective. Everything else comes second.

Alignment of Self and Soul

I am a human being between birth and death, but within me lies a connector to infinite Life itself, or God. From this connection with cosmic life arises my duty. I must strive to align my so-called self – the individual identity who screams, 'ME, ME, ME!' – with the real self which is connected through my soul to cosmic life itself. I must align my ego-self with my spiritual self, with my soul. The alignment will bring about the realisation that the so-called ego-self is only an indicator to the soul. In itself it has no independent reality or sustainability. It is only there to point you towards the soul. It is a lie that points towards the truth.

My duty and responsibility in this life is to make sure that these two are in full alignment. I can then take appropriate care of the temporary changes in my transient environment, without forgetting to constantly acknowledge the source of my sentience, feelings, and emotions: the spirit within me.

Self-Reflection Questions:

1. Describe an incident when you lost control of your feelings or emotions? Consider how it could have been different had you been in balance or alignment?

❧ Now take responsibility for what you have learned and apply it toward future challenging situations

2. Reflect upon a time when you experienced being in harmony with your soul?

Chapter Four

The Rise to Higher Consciousness

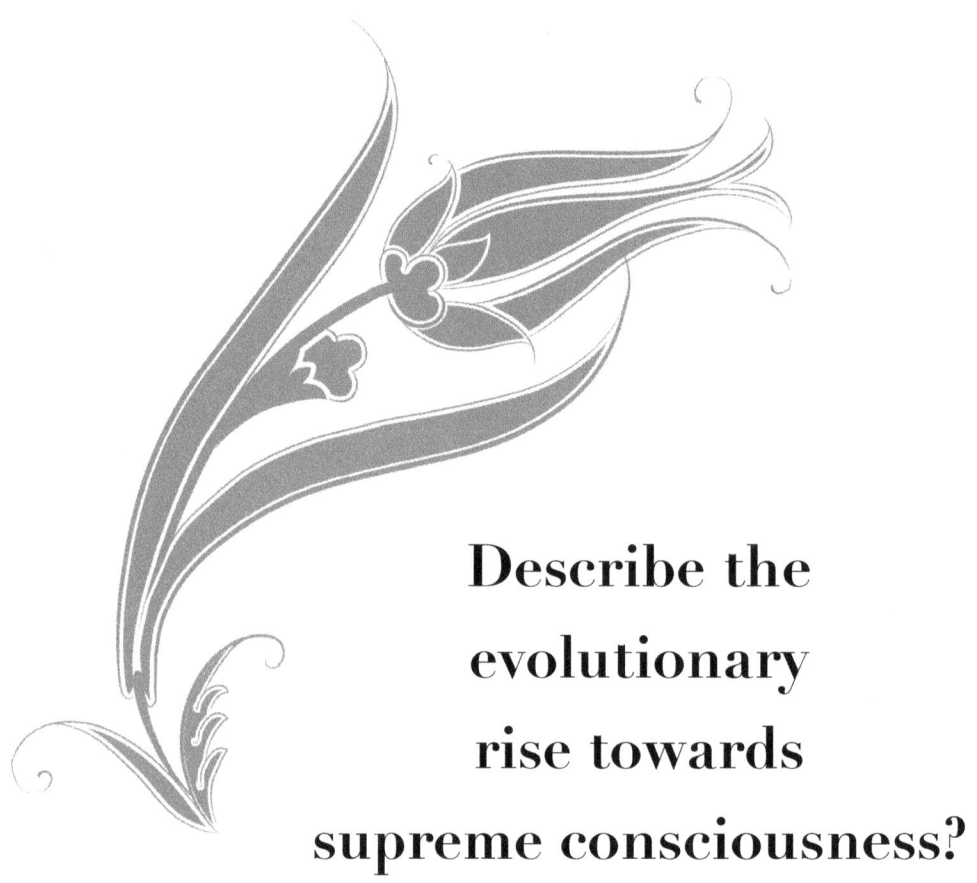

Describe the evolutionary rise towards supreme consciousness?

The Evolutionary Rise of Consciousness

It all began with absolute, infinite, and boundless energy. In a fraction of the first second of the big bang, the plans and patterns of everything that came over billions of years were already set in place. The whole story was present in that first touch. This is why science tries to duplicate and replicate the first intense moment where everything was in that boundless energy field without differentiation. Within that millionth of a second everything began to happen: from the galactic to the quantum, the outer and the inner, the known and the unknown. We are all connected, albeit unconsciously. We all emerged from, and connect to, that moment when there was only supreme consciousness.

Once creation began, infinite varieties of connections, attractions, repulsions, and consciousness began to occur. The same is true for each human being. The newly born baby has basic consciousness which develops over time with the help of the mother and others until it can express itself. Much of what we express as we grow reveals our desire to return to tranquillity and peace. Peace was the origin of it all. There was nothing until that first, immense moment, which set every pattern, pressure, and priority in place.

The memory of that origin is in each of us. It lies within our spirit and soul. However, we are more affected and influenced by short-term memory; by what happened yesterday and all the destruction and fire of last week, and whatever we perceive as close to us in time. We have short-, medium- and long-term memory, but all of them are due to an original, primal memory, which arises from original, pure consciousness.

Once life takes on a specific form or body, then it is subject to the evolutionary move towards higher consciousness. The baby, child, and teenager want to know, explore, and discover. Knowledge is a connector between the seen and the unseen, between cause and effect. We all want to relate and understand, for then there will be peace. If you understand it, then your mind is at rest. You no longer investigate which came first or second; which is more prominent; which is more dominant and so on.

We have the five senses to help us in that exploration. They are like five different torches which shine upon a situation. These five senses all connect. Sight, sound, touch, smell, and taste connect with each other. We have the most amazingly complex, instant analysis and reports from the laboratories within ourselves that perform thousands of tests just to tell us that this smell is not the same as the other. Life as we know it now evolved over a few million years from a mix of seawater and mineral deposits exposed to just the right conditions into complex human beings capable of being aware of awareness.

The unseen and unknown is the other half of our story, and it dominates this little half with its appearances and experiences, its planets and galaxies and systems and stars. All that we can discern manifests from the infinite unknown for a while, completes its circuitry changes – up and down, strange and beautiful, millions of years or a billionth of a second – and then returns to the pure cosmic light.

Self- Reflection Questions

1. Reflect upon an incident when you were able to shift toward higher consciousness. What were the factors that enabled you to make this shift?

    - Acknowledge those factors and apply them toward the rise to higher consciousness.

2. Describe the lessons you learned about yourself.

Chapter Five

The Perpetual Now

What is the perpetual 'Now' - how does it connect to timelessness?

The Perpetual Now

The present moment is timeless. How can we say that?

Duality is a central characteristic of the material world. If there is time, then there is timelessness. If there is the experience of a movement within space and time, then there must be its opposite. One side cannot exist without the other: this is the nature of duality.

Yet, where is it that we find no space or time, no movement, no Big Bang or Collapse?

That state is already here, in the perpetual now. It is here for us to touch and calibrate with, giving us the appropriate perspective of space and time. Embracing the perpetual now is touching the zone of timelessness in you. This zone is that of our spirit or soul, which is not within time and space, yet it gives rise to time and space. It has produced our feeling and understanding of time, where we have been trained to expect cyclical continuity, day in and day out, as night turns into day, and as we journey around the sun every year.

For instance, certain fruit may only grow in specific seasons. Now may not be the right season for growth, so we must wait for the change in weather. This understanding forces us to put things into perspective regarding change, timing, and appropriateness.

The journey of the spirit or the soul is one that occurs within space and time, yet the spirit or the soul is from a zone of timelessness. The confinement in conditioned consciousness means that we must constantly calibrate and consider the moment. We must understand what is happening, how it is happening, what the temperature is, how other people are responding, and whether they are friends or foes, so that we are prepared to perform our primary duty, which is to be in constant adoration and obsession with Life.

This is the primary driving force in existence: to maintain and continue life. Everything that we do, always, is to do with that. Whether it is pursuing pleasure, health or wealth, each act is an attempt to ensure the continuation of our life. Life itself is ever continuous. Once we know that life is not separate from Life itself, which is ever continuous, then the fear of death and sorrow about death will fall away.

Self-Reflection Questions:

1. What does it mean to you to be in the Now?

    - Adopt the practice of putting aside opinion and judgment, and remain open and receptive to the moment.

2. How does that affect your perspective or attitude towards life?

Chapter Six

The Driving Forces in Life

What are the major driving forces in life?

The Major Driving Forces in Life

As intelligent human beings seeking peace and contentment in this life, there are numerous attributes that we wish to attain and experience. These desirable attributes, such as generosity, kindness, love, affection, goodness, all help us to flow towards infinite Life itself. Yet even attributes which are considered as positive come with their equivalent shadows. These negative attributes, considered to be vices, are ones which we wish to shun.

The reason for liking positive attributes and disliking negative ones is quite simple. The positive attributes help us to move faster, better, and more smoothly along the evolutionary arc of the rise of consciousness. The negative ones, such as meanness and fear, stop us from flowing into the zone of our own soul, which is eternal and cosmic. All human drives, attractions and repulsions fall along the natural rise in consciousness from lower, limited, and conditioned consciousness towards higher consciousness.

This natural rise is repeatedly shown to us, even in the pure biography of a child. From a small amount of consciousness, step by step, through the teenage years and into maturity, we are always moving towards higher values and consciousness. As we grow older, we are no longer interested only in the pure material, physical, tangible, edible, and touchable. We want to experience higher states because that is the nature of our soul. There is a natural drive from lower to higher consciousness. There is an evolution in and of the human condition. The present human is much more advanced in consciousness than two hundred years ago. This may not necessarily be good or bad as this is cyclical and depends on how we choose to use that consciousness.

Continuity

The rise in human consciousness is ever continuing. Human beings a hundred years ago were far more conscious and aware than two thousand years ago. Similarly, humans of today are more conscious and aware than those who lived a hundred years ago. We have moved from a basic, primitive state towards one which is more conducive to awakening to the light of our own soul or source within each of us. Increasingly, we want to be at one with the One. This implies that we are experiencing different facets of life, but our drive is towards pure, ongoing, continuous, and eternal Life itself, which are qualities of the divine, Supreme Consciousness or God. It is for this reason that we are driven to any experience or any state that is perpetual and eternal.

This explains why we question whether any relationship is long-lasting, implying a desire for it to be closer to that which is forever. We want situations or relationships that are durable because life itself is the most durable. Life is eternal, but not my life. I am here to grasp the importance of time as to transcend it into the timelessness of life itself. If I have not done that, then I fear death and I have not completed my journey. If I have done it, then I also appreciate conditioned and limited life as a manifestation of infinite, perpetual, eternal Life itself.

The same applies to aspects of our contentment and happiness. That is why a mature human being does not dwell upon any pleasure that will change in time. We like to have pleasurable and relaxed situations, but these are samples that drive us to question what durable contentment and happiness is and how this state may be cultivated. It is not just about touching it for five minutes and then paying a price for five years. I am driven to tap into a zone that is bliss with nothing else in it – eternal paradise.

Consciousness

Metaphorically, Adam was born in paradise, where there were no needs. However, his ignorance of his state anticipated his fall into duality, which means needs and fulfilling needs, so as to return consciously to that which is forever. The soul of Adam was forever, but the idea or concept in the mind of Adam of foreverness did not exist. The Abrahamic religions say that the promise that you can now be 'forever' is the whisper of the lower self. As soon as Adam falls for this, the Real answer comes, 'No, you cannot pretend here in the realm of absolute perfection of Oneness. You must enter the world of duality, hanging on air, where there is good and bad, and all is temporary. You must experience the good and the bad and the up and the down.'

We all want to get out of this constant yoyoing. We seek perpetual perfection, which is the nature of our own soul. The only way we can experience this is by transcending conditioned consciousness through peace, quiet, meditation, prayers, hope, crying, and so on, until we enter that zone of utter silence which is the doorway to utter perfection. On this earth we are localised beings, striving to attain our origin, which is universality and Absoluteness. We are here but aiming to be there, or wherever it is that the possibility of space or time no longer exists. No four dimensions. Just is. That is the nature of our own soul. All our aspirations, hopes, prayers, and training in this life is for us to be able to – by will – touch that zone of supreme consciousness, which is the nature of our own soul or spirit.

It is the manifestation of what we call Supreme Consciousness, the Divine, God, the Absolute, or whatever name you happen to prefer. Our only connection with the Absolute is through what we call Life. It is an amazing cosmic force that is everywhere, always. Life forces are really to do with that which is within space and time and the realm of human experience. These forces propel us to experience more widely and deeply.

There are life forces towards which we are attracted. Forces we are repulsed from are the shadows of the forces to which we are attracted. We are attracted to what in ethics are called 'desirables,' or virtues: generosity, goodness, kindness, knowledge and so on. Their shadows are the reverse: meanness, darkness, ignorance and so on.

However, what we term as 'lower consciousness' is not to be derided or discarded. It is our earthly existence. It is what Adam is here to experience. It is the main part of our energy and personality, of you and me. We are on earth; we cannot deny that. As earthly creatures, drawing energy from our unearthly or heavenly side, which is the soul, we are constantly veering towards the idea of benefit.

In the last few hundred years, benefit has become purely materialistic. Five hundred years ago, benefit referred more to being in tune with the innermost, elevated in transcendence, and all the other spiritual experiences people had as part of their day-to-day life. As we learned to harness external sources of power and began the agricultural revolution, then the industrial revolution, then more efficient means of warfare and so on, we became established on this main track which has resulted in all of us being conditioned with the idea that 'more is better.' By this thought, we only cheat ourselves.

The more you have in an outer sense, even of knowledge, the less you have of higher, inner knowledge. It is as simple as that. The two are always balanced. The more self-awareness you have, the less soul-awareness. You need to have self-awareness, but only to transcend it. If it is just 'self! self! self!' then you become your own walking biography. This is how people suffer, and we are designed by our soul, which is the provider of all energy, not wanting to suffer.

Consciousness, Connectedness, Continuity

Connection to the infinite is sometimes called 'pure joy', 'bliss', 'boundless happiness' or 'God's presence'. There are hundreds of names given to that which all of us desire and long for. It is the quality of the soul that we love and adore.

Once we are in conditionality, as we all are, then that infinite, boundless bliss or joy becomes dimmed. The more we participate in cause and effect, up and down, like and dislike, the less we experience the wonderful gift of pure joy for its own sake. For example, I am now in the zone of duality and joy because of something. I am hungry, so I eat and say 'I am very pleased' because I am no longer experiencing the pain of hunger. This is a sample of that zone of contentment and pleasure which is boundless.

I am being nurtured along that path towards the infinite that is ever there. But I am not there! I am occupied with a specific end product, or some food, or an achievement, or making money, or whatever. All of this distracts from the natural flow which is beyond mind and human aspiration or desires.

Our drive is always towards higher consciousness because higher consciousness leads us to the edge of the limiting box of space and time. Since the soul or the spirit is neither bound nor limited by space and time, and since our reality is that spirit, we are naturally driven to a zone of experience which is at the edge of transcending space and time. Higher consciousness is awareness of the changes and limitations within space and time, which is simultaneously directly connected with that which is infinite and boundless, or the

Absolute. To want to touch this is a natural drive for anything that is aware of Life. Once awareness of awareness occurs, a drive to go beyond all local awareness and beyond all universal awareness into Pure Awareness surges.

As for connection and continuity, there is nothing ever in the universe that is disconnected. It is a question of the extent of visible, discernible connections to which we can refer, in combination with increasingly subtle connections which may be less obvious. All and everything are connected, but my little plant here in this pot, for example, is obviously more connected to the soil, air, and water around it than to the soil, air, and water that is one thousand kilometres away. There is both locality in connection and there is universality in connection.

Continuity points to timelessness. Everything within our space and time sphere, within our little universe, will return to its origin, its destiny, in the one cosmic Reality. Neither origin nor end is bound by space and time. The experience of this reality beyond space and time is what we continually and perpetually yearn for. That is why no human being at any time, in the normal sense of consciousness, is content or happy.

Following on from this is the drive toward durable contentment and the wellbeing of body, mind, and heart. It can also be explained as the drive toward the edge of consciousness. If I have pain, I am programmed (consciously and otherwise) to reduce the pain, because it is a warning that my consciousness of life may be lost, and I am obsessed with consciousness of life. My system focuses me to take care of that pain, hunger, danger, or need.

Such needs are not only physical. As you move higher in consciousness, one must similarly focus on emotional needs and so on, until you enter the subtler realms of spiritual needs. To experience these realms is to recharge and be in touch with your own spirit constantly. In fact, the truth is that you *are* the spirit, but you have accumulated other layers on it, such as its shadow or so-called ego or animal self, which has been earthly for millions of years and now is connected with this heavenly zone of your own spirit.

The issue of contentment is the same as that of stability. If you are fully, totally content in every way, then there is no drive to experience anything in life. You are either a stone, or dead, or are now transcending your human limitations. True contentment and happiness is found at the edge of transcendence where you are now absent from visible, physical, material realities. You are now at the edge of the Source of all these realities. One may call it the Universal Primordial Soup in which everything is, though nothing may be discernible. Matter and antimatter balance each other perfectly, with everything and nothing. That is the story of the Void. If you go up a thousand kilometres into the air, there is no air. You cannot hear. It is empty. It behaves like a vacuum, but it is from this same vacuum that everything has emerged.

Locality - Universality

Locality and universality has to do with space and time. Local is something near to me as I measure. I have a body, an arm, a finger. I have limitations in my little personal kingdom. Anything that is within reach, which influences me at any minute, is 'local' and I must be aware of the local, because I am obsessed with life and its preservation. I want to know whether the roof is going to fall on me or not, therefore I am concerned and cautious with the local. This is where my limited ability to control, affect and change applies.

However, I am not in any way disconnected from the universal. Consider sunspots. Cooler areas on the sun's surface cause a reorganisation in the magnetic field lines near them, which result in solar flares. These bursts of solar radiation interact with the electromagnetic field of the Earth, affecting everything from the way birds navigate to the electronics in your phone. A meteorite falls five thousand miles away and, if it is big enough, it will cause the sky to darken for a year, which immediately affects everything. Locality exists as a little reminder of space and time, but it is an aspect of universality. The two are intimately connected.

Self-Reflection Questions

1. Consider a time when you felt deeply connected to something or someone?

2. Reflect upon your experience of interconnectedness?

3. Reflect upon the drive of continuity and how it occurs in your life experience.

4. What changes can you make in your life that may reduce suffering and bring about more durable states of equilibruim?

   - Identify one thing that you can act upon today to reduce suffering or bring about more durable balance and harmony?

Chapter Seven

Certainty and Uncertainty

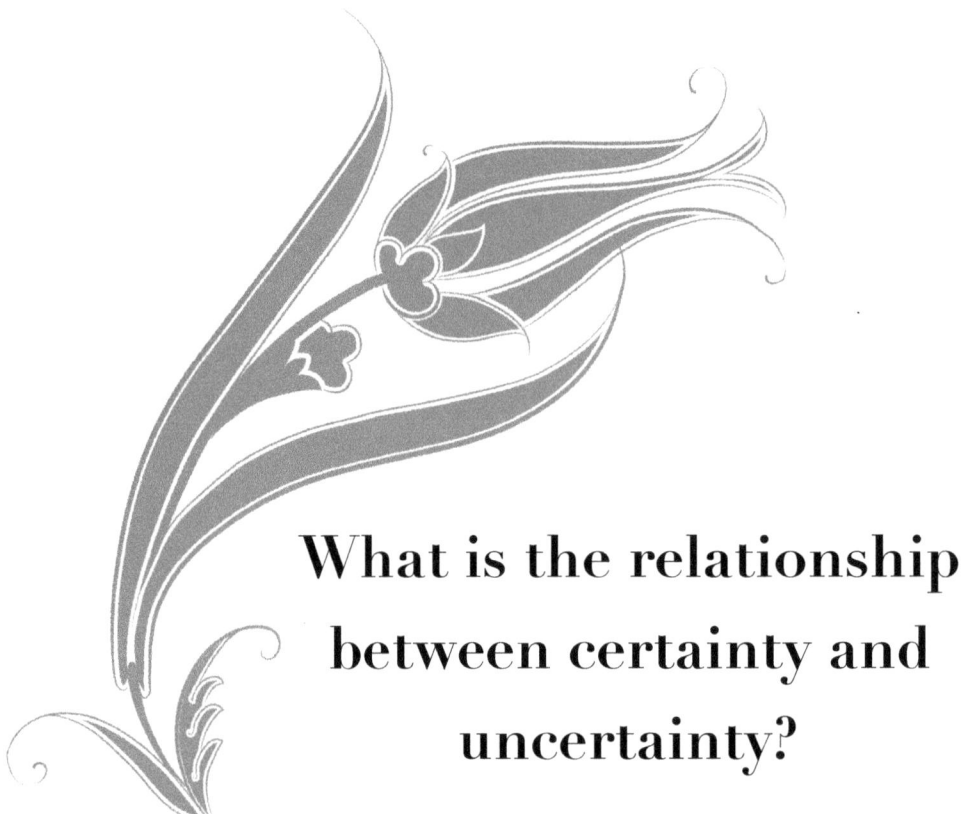

What is the relationship between certainty and uncertainty?

Drive towards certainty

A major drive of life is to be certain, secure, and to know that one is safe and not in danger. Without that drive for safety and security, there would be no growth in human beings, civilization, and cultures. You would not work. What is the point of working, earning, and making a lovely home and garden, if you know that tomorrow you will be raided and invaded and all of it will be lost? You would have no incentive to do anything, unless you know there is reasonable safety, security, and certainty.

However, all our desires for certainty and security are challenged by continual change. After all everything is in flux. Even mountains are moving all the time, albeit a few centimetres a year. Go away for ten thousand years and you may find that where you were standing there is now a mountain, or an island in what was once the middle of the ocean.

Durable Certainty

Real certainty is to do with a zone of experience that is not subject to space or time. Beyond space and time is another level of durable, reliable certainty. Once it descends into the limitations of space and time, then its certainty and security are limited. The closer it gets to a living entity like us, the more uncertain and insecure it becomes. Transience honours human beings because it gives us urgency to experience space and time: we deal with what is within it, and then transcend it by entering silence, into the Original Peace.

The knowledge that any certainty, reliability or peace within space and time is hazy and short-lived and that anything can change in any minute drives us beyond what we think to be secure or insecure. In fact, all that we consider as our most reliable, durable investments are entirely transient. You are yourself hanging on air! The air that goes in may not come out. If, for a few moments, you are cut off from oxygen you will lose your mental faculties.

All is temporary and yet for us to interact with the world outside we need to have a certain measure of it being not too temporary. If we know anything is going to disappear in the next minute, we would not do anything! Yet we must interact with this world, because this is our nursery. This is our playground where we take things seriously and then realise that they are not, in the end, that serious. Even life and death are not that serious, because Life continues forever. What is timeless and boundless is more durable than whatever we experience in our world.

Self-Reflection Questions

1. How does the experience of uncertainty affect your perspective on life?

2. How can experiencing higher consciousness help you deal with uncertainty?

    ﮋ	Identify a "tool" that could facilitate the shift to higher consciousness.

Chapter Eight

The Teacher and the Seeker

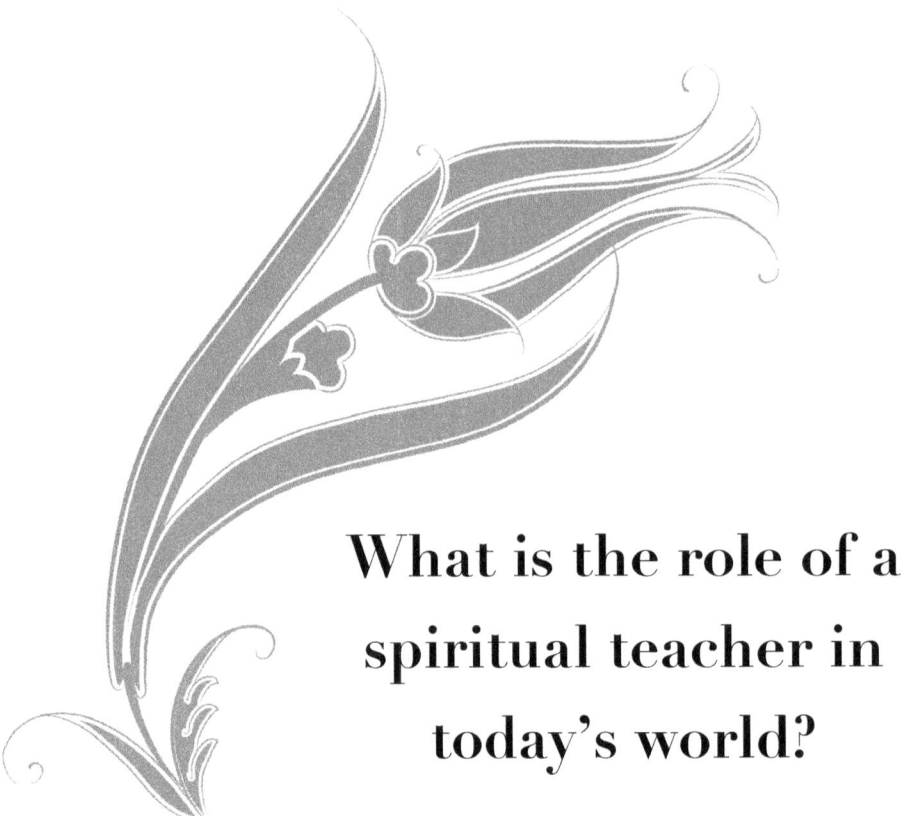

What is the role of a spiritual teacher in today's world?

Can you describe the healthy expectations of a seeker?

Drive Toward Awakening

We are all seekers. Every human being wants a better life. No matter where, or who you are, even if you are a so-called realised or awakened being, you still have hopes, expectations, and desires. They may not be the same as the hopes, expectations, and desires of the person who is greedy and wants to accumulate all the wealth they can, but you still have some desire. For example: the desire that Mercy will become more visible to all, or that Divine Presence will become obvious to everyone, or that our interference with other living creatures will become less abusive than it is in today's culture.

The global population is now at a point where we are close to eight billion people and have choked our earth with pollution that has reduced the quality of our environment. We have damaged our natural habitat that has existed and coasted along for billions of years – what we call the 'flow of nature'. We have interfered to such an extent that we are now living in a zone where human interruption and unnatural selection is prevalent. Yet, everybody is hopeful and wants to have the best. Everybody wants to awaken to a zone that is always reliable, secure, and certain. Human consciousness straddles the source of pure cosmic consciousness and ever-changing shadows, moment to moment.

Role of the Teacher

Historically, the issue of having a master or a teacher was vital. It had been so from the time that settlements appeared, ten or twelve thousand years ago, even before agriculture. There were always people within the tribe, village, or town, who were awakened to a higher zone of consciousness. They were identified as godly or divine people and were revered. Much of this has evaporated in our world over the last two or three decades.

There have always been people who give less importance or attention to their day-to-day experiences and are far more connected with the vast, infinite, unseen and unknown. Their inner condition is more in tune with that which is timeless. Their wisdom, what they say and do, and what they consider to be important, will still be relevant in many hundreds of years to come.

The teacher and disciple relationship has been an important one. Now that our knowledge has become almost exclusively secular and of a basic, low grade, scientific kind, these relationships are less and less important. The teacher can be anybody who knows more than you, who can act as a reference or mirror for you. They can calibrate your work, direction, concern, and needs.

There are two angles to the teacher and disciple relationship. One is a seeker's point of view: you want to have a reliable spiritual encyclopaedia who will enable you to move onwards, rather than getting stuck in a spiritual personality. From the seeker's viewpoint, you need a teacher who is not expecting anything from you; one who is free of you. You, however, are not free of him or her. You are still encumbered by your own emotions, feelings, and phobias, because you are obsessed with life.

The teacher would also have a point of view. An awakened teacher is living life itself, without the personal gravitational pull of it. Life itself is free: life is Life is life. They know what level of evolution, in terms of consciousness, the seeker is at so he or she is not over-burdened or under-stimulated. The teacher also knows that the seeker is always given encouragement along their wayfaring until they realise that everything originated from Supreme Consciousness. Everything has descended to us from Oneness.

This is not about comparing subjective experiences, an act which is only relevant when you are under water. When you are above water, you are no longer concerned about how far you are from fully awakening. Fully awakened light is already there, everywhere, including in the darkness. In the absence of the traditional concept of a teacher, one may find insight and guidance from the lessons and mirrors given by the tiniest creatures or short encounters with different people in differing circumstances. Teaching comes when you are committed to your own awakening, with openness, humility and sincerity. When beams of light, however thin, penetrate veils of darkness, the Light that is already present becomes illuminated, even if by a glimpse.

Self-Reflection Questions

1. If there is someone whom you consider as a teacher or reference: what qualities do they exhibit that are valuable?

    - Identify three or four of their qualities. How are they linked to your behaviour, thoughts or actions?

2. If you have a spiritual guide or mentor in your life, consider the qualities you bring to the relationship?

Chapter Nine

Levels of Consciousness

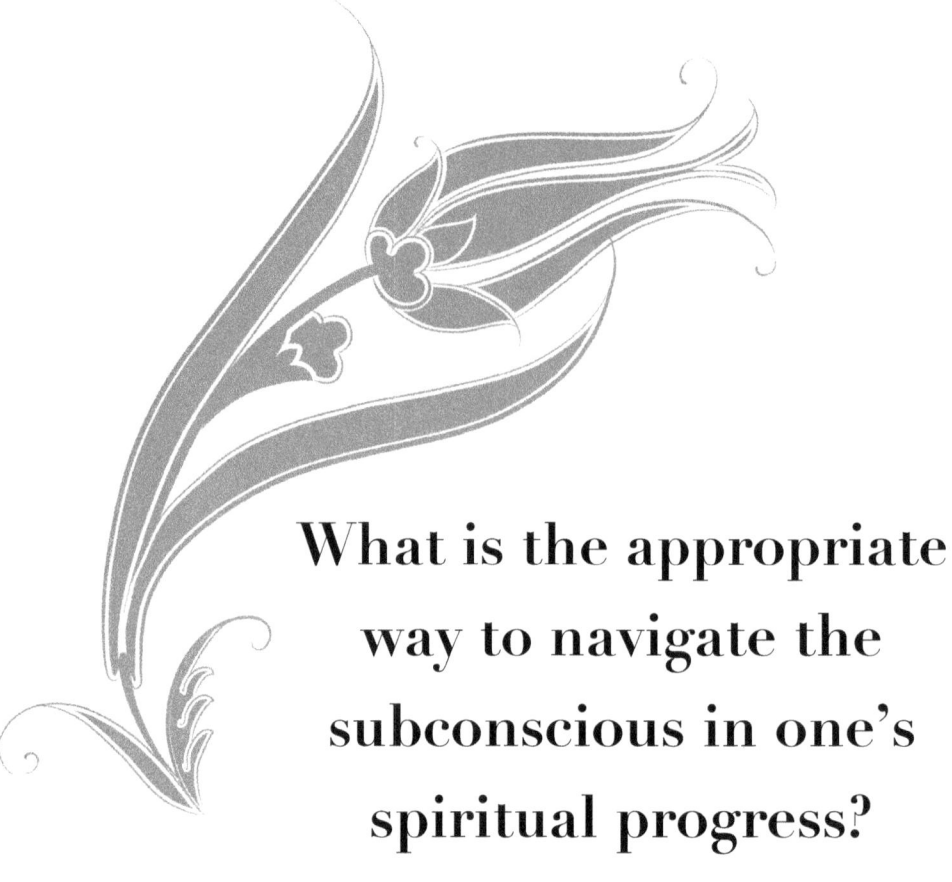

What is the appropriate way to navigate the subconscious in one's spiritual progress?

What guidance can you give to a seeker who is struggling with emotional and mental patterns and limitations?

Levels of Conscious Experience

This question is about the journey from childhood to maturity through numerous levels and zones of consciousness.

We are all within the confines of space and time. While the soul or spirit manifests in a manner within space and time, its nature and life are not conditioned by space and time. The answer really is that we human beings, or any other creatures, have no option other than to accept our limitations and the limits of our sensory abilities to receive and transmit any signal or experience. In this regard we are all limited.

The truth is that Life is a celestial, heavenly reality manifesting on earth. That is what it is. It is the connection between the infinite and the finite, and the Absolute and the limited or relative. We experience numerous levels and zones of consciousness in our lives. How many strands are there within the subconscious, within sleep consciousness, within pain consciousness, and on and on? This is part of the human cosmology and make up which has been evolving over millions of years.

To put these levels of our conscious experience into the right perspective, we need to constantly recalibrate and take reference from the zone of Full Consciousness in us. We can only do this through first stopping and transcending limited consciousness by entering silence: that doorway into a deep, indescribable, meditative state. Then you are in the neutral zone in which you may experience touches of the Boundless from which everything has emerged.

A key point to highlight is the danger of falling into the trap of words like 'enlightenment' or 'awakening' that so-called seekers use without being embedded in the meaning of the numerous cultures from which they are borrowed, whether it is Hindu, Buddhist, Christian, Islamic or other distinct spiritual pathways. There are many cultural names that are often used to indicate the state of awakening or epiphanies, but without an understanding and appreciation of the cultural context these can cause confusion. They were part of a different model that was used sometime in the past when distinct paths existed. Groups and communities were concerned with questions of linguistic and cultural belonging. It is my personal experience that, though these terms are interesting to touch upon and understand, trying to return to that culture is like a modern person trying to dress up in the armour-plating used by the crusaders. It does not work. That had its own day, its own culture. We are not in that state. It is really by silence, by stillness – holding it here – that one will be recharged by the Absolute Source of everything we know and all we do not know.

Self-Reflection Questions

1. Reflect upon what you consider to be the limiting blockages to higher consciousness, and how you can overcome them.

   - Act on one or two of the limiting blockages today and begin to resolve them.

2. Reflect upon your relationship with stillness and silence.

Chapter Ten

The Question of Free Will

Is there free will or is everything predestined?

How does that relate to responsibility and actions?

The Question of Free Will

As reasonably healthy and intelligent human beings we know that the most fundamental part of day-to-day experience relates to action and reaction. If I am not careful about where I am walking, I may fall with the force of gravity pulling me down causing damage to my limbs. If I eat too much, I may get indigestion. If I do not take care of my health and breathe good air, I may get sick. There is a balance in all consequences: action and reaction, up and down, matter and antimatter.

Everything is in balance, so my free will is neither free, nor is it personal. However, for everyday talk one can say, 'Yes, you have free will: you can lift your arm, or not. If, after many days of demanding work without rest, you would like to sleep, you can.' You have needs and desires on numerous levels: physical, biological, hormonal, chemical, emotional, spiritual. Each of these various levels have their balanced state. In fact, there is a demand to be in balance, because if you are not in balance, you are denying reception and transmission, which is giving and taking. The whole business of existence is about connecting: give and take, hear and respond, my will and God's.

If I am not in balance, I am missing the most fundamental part of a basic, healthy life. Once the balance is established, it is possible to see how we both have a free will and how everything is predestined. If I rely on a roof when the weather is changing all the time but I do not attend to its maintenance, it is destined to fall. I must exercise my will by understanding and acknowledging that it is time for this roof to be changed or reinforced. Everything has a destiny. If my personal will or free will works along the way of improving destiny towards stability, goodness, and reliability, then I am exercising my will in an evolutionarily balanced way.

If not, then I am abusing the stewardship allocated to me in this life as a responsible member of the living creatures on this tiny earth of ours. How responsibly I function as a steward here indicates the extent to which I have been trained in Cosmic Mastery, Absolute Power, or God's governance of the whole cosmos. I am not separate from that. So, if I reflect that state in the best possible and most correct way, then I cause less damage to myself and others, especially in terms of the misery, sorrow, and fears that I project. This is important, because nature does not want us to bring about catastrophic changes, which we have been doing to a great extent in recent times.

You have free will in a very tiny sphere or space. In truth, everything has a destiny and even your free will is a part of that overall destiny.

Self-Reflection Questions

1. Consider how exercising your will connects to experiencing the best destiny?

    - Assess three different decisions that you made over the past two or three years. Include what you now believe to be right or wrong decisions. Consider the decree you knew then and what you know now, that impacted on your decision. Now re-assess each decision in a way that you see only the good in it.

2. Consider how you exercise responsible stewardship in your relationships with others, the environment, and yourself?

Chapter Eleven

Personal Will and Destiny

Would you talk about fusing personal will with Cosmic will?

Alignment of Personal Will with Divine Will

There is one Source from which all known and unknown powers emerge, and that is called Divine Will. Divine Will manifests according to a full spectrum, the ultimate pinnacle of which is to fully be integrated with Divine Will itself.

But the way it happens is, initially there is this illusion of separateness and independence, and therefore it is easy to conclude that you can do A, B and C. I can choose. But this is a very low level of intelligence. With a bit of higher intelligence, you will want to choose that which does not want to harm you in the future. With yet a bit more higher intelligence, you will want to choose that which flows along the flow of nature, which is one of the most powerful agents of the Divine. So in truth, there is only Divine Will. Higher intelligence will take you to a point where you don't want to plan, think, or act, unless it is within the movement of Divine Will. Then you have no sorrow, no fear, no anxiety.

There is seamlessness in the universe. It is only with our feeble minds that we see differentiation.

Every situation exists along a spectrum. At one end it is discernible, chemical, physical, material. I experience it as personal: 'This is my leg! That is your head.' However, the total situation includes not just my experience, but others' too. One end is personal, the other is communal. One end is local, the other is universal. One end is temporary and relative – time passes, and this minute is different from the last – the other end is Absolute, which we also call God.

The Illusion of Independence

The personal end contains the illusion that I have independence, the illusion that I can do things on my own. But we never stop to ask, 'Where did I get that ability from? Where does my supposed power or energy come from?' It is for this reason the world is in the mess that it is. Everybody believes that they can do whatever they want, pretending to be demigods. Acting in this way leads to greater suffering, increasing our fear of death because once we die, we are no longer in this theatre playing our own miserable role, thinking that we are the author. You have been given the short-term license to function as a messenger, as an actor, but you are not the author.

Everything is fused in the unseen and the unknown. It is only the identity you have been practicing from babyhood which sees separation and thinks: 'I can do this, I can fight others, I can cry, I can scream, I can throw a tantrum and my poor parents will run because the neighbours will complain.' All these miserable illusions of ours are shadows of shadows of shadows and here we are talking about the light of God!

The local and the universal, the temporary and the constant, are all brackets of a spectrum which has no beginning and no end. No time and non-time. It is ever there. That is why we say there is only God. There is only that utter, Absolute Truth from which numerous universes have emerged, each contained within a certain time and space and set of personal limitations which make us believe it to be our universe.

With intelligence one accepts these limiting conditions and learns how to celebrate limitation. You have the capacity of a miraculous treasure, but you are chasing after small little pebbles. We must go through the pebble phase before discovering that the ultimate mine of precious gems was already there. Why then are you going to mine it? Where are you going to take them? What are you going to do with them all?

We must change our attitude to our roles and position in life altogether. Higher intelligence tells us that we will not change an iota of what we are seeing, including the suffering! Such intelligence is rare. Until it becomes common, it will be a battle which everyone wants to cheat. The whole business is about cheating, because you have been cheated by the illusion of who you are. That is the ultimate, fundamental cheat.

Until this realisation sinks in, the earth cannot sustain us. All this business around anxiety, fear, and suffering, whether internal or external due to situations like climate change, will only get worse, because we think we can control it by carrying on in the same framework as before. It is not possible. It is a lie.

Self-Reflection Questions

1. Consider the roles you play on broader levels: Family, Community, Universal.

    - What actions can you take on each of the three levels to align with the Cosmic will more closely?

2. What do you understand by cosmic will? How does that relate to your personal will and the roles you play?

3. What does it mean to you to be aligned with Cosmic/Divine will?

Chapter Twelve

Presence

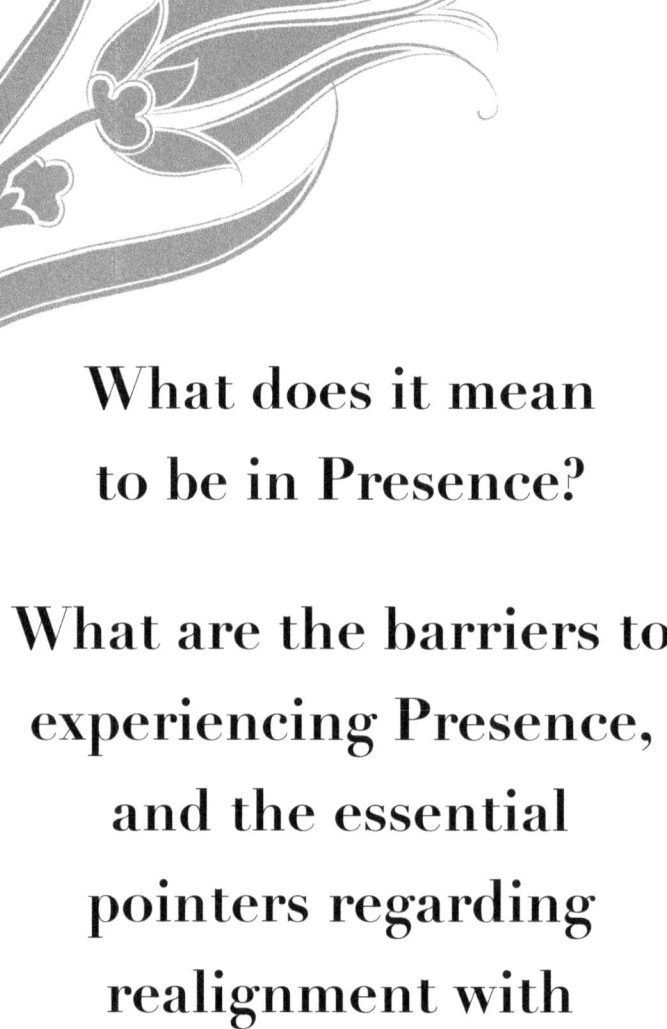

What does it mean to be in Presence?

What are the barriers to experiencing Presence, and the essential pointers regarding realignment with Presence?

Being Present

In its final stage Presence is timelessness. If you are in the now, right *now*, you will know that *now* is forever. If you are fully, totally in the present, with no discernible traces of the past or concern about the future, then you are truly, fully in Presence. Being present implies neutrality. It also means, in an emotional sense, indifference: you have no desires, fears, sorrows, or attachments. When you are present you are at the edge of entering into full silence, which is Timeless and Eternal. It is from here that everything in existence has emerged – from Cosmic Silence.

Before entering that zone of Presence, one is caught between dualities – cause and effect, up and down, good and bad, attracting and repelling. This is our condition in minute-to-minute everyday life; you are actively trying to maintain balance, because you are in the zone of conditioned consciousness. If you want to rise further and touch the flow as a conscious step on this unavoidable journey we all take towards higher consciousness, then you need to know how to exit your conditioned consciousness, even amid your ever-changing activities.

Our soul is a hologram of Supreme Consciousness, but our mind and its application in our day-to-day activity operates within the zone of conditioned consciousness. Absence from the individuated 'separate' self reveals Presence. You need to stop, switch off the engine, switch off everything. Now you are in between full, infinite consciousness and its emergence as conditioned consciousness.

Self-Reflection Questions

1. Consider what it means to be fully present?
   - Reflect on a time when you experienced being in the present moment. Identify the characteristics or feelings that defined being fully present?
2. What does it mean to you to be in presence?

Chapter Thirteen

Death and Eternal Life

What happens after death?

The Illusion of Our Biography

The issue one must begin with is birth because whatever begins will end. Nothing comes into time unless it also leaves the measurement of the illusion of time. If I have identified myself with my biography and think: 'This is me, here I am,' then I have failed to realise that this 'me' is only a minor aspect of the real me. It is a picture which changes every day. If you are in a bad mood, take a picture. If you are happy, take another. Which picture is the real you?

What happened at birth is a miracle if you know that its mirror image occurs at death. Pure cosmic energy, or God, transmits an infinite range of energy fields into the material end of the spectrum, resulting in the inception of a life, be it a mouse or a human being. That cosmic energy, which we call spirit or soul, enters a zone on earth and gives it lifeforce, which then appears as its life. Why does it appear as its life? Because the mystery of life is such that it only perpetuates itself. The mystery of life is that Life perpetuates life.

There is only Life

We are all obsessed with Life. If one has been touched, your obsession with life may even lead you to kill other people to maintain your life, until you know that, in truth, there is only Life and whatever there is emanates from Life. That is why you say, 'There is only God.' There is only Life!

The amazingly complex human mechanism is made up of the most intricately connected cosmology of cells, neurons, organs, faculties, and senses, which lead to will, mind, and the unconscious, subconscious, and conscious experience of the so-called you. What happens at death is that the instrument which kept life on earth, your self, ceases to operate. It stops being differentiated. It returns to where it belongs: all the minerals and all the elements return into the Earth and the Light back to its origin.

There are trace elements of all kinds, even gold, in every human being. All the elements that exist also exist in us. Death is just the completion of the cycle. This bundle of divine energy, the soul, spirit or *rūh*, is everywhere, always, as the carrier of life that energises matter into being 'me'. Just like energy and matter, I am inseparable from my soul in the same way that I am inseparable from my hand until you sever my hand, and it returns to its earthiness and inertness.

What happens after death is that the soul or spirit returns to what it has always been and is now. When I was alive, it was partially given the colour of 'me' but no longer.

A Natural Continuation of Consciousness

Death has always been considered the natural conclusion of the first journey of any living being, whether human, rat, or cat. A natural continuation of higher energy, consciousness, and life without the encumberment of the body or wider physical limitations, like walls, ceilings, and changing temperatures. From the earliest times, most human cultures have respected the need for certain provisions and special considerations for 'the journey' after death. These older cultures knew that there is a second experience after leaving the body.

The body was also considered sacred because it houses the sacred soul. What happens after death is that the so-called you, which is a combination of the rūh or spirit and its experiences on earth, gets purified of these experiences so that the soul may return to Original Purity. There is a period after death which many cultures and religions, especially those of the Abrahamic lineage, recognise as that within which the rūh is purified and moves on.

However, the experiential traces we carry are still in the zone of time and space after death and continue, but not in the same proportion as the time and space we experienced when we are alive. Experiencing the repercussions of our wrongdoing or good work stretches out towards eternity. Therefore, we experience either hellish conditions – burning and purifying – or gardenic conditions of flow and the joy of being the *rūh* consciously, which is divine.

Self-Reflection Questions

1. Consider your understanding of the continuation of life?

2. What is your understanding of the next phase of life?

3. How does that affect your attitude and behaviour in this life?

    - Spend time considering your own death before prayer or meditation. Use the reflection gained through this to purify your intention in your prayer. When you find you are acting inappropriately, remember death and reframe your intention. Carry out this exercise for a day.

Chapter Fourteen

Service, Identity and Belonging

What would be an acceptable way to serve and contribute to society, and how does this relate to truth and the drive towards higher consciousness?

Service, Identity and Belonging

Everything has emerged from One and returns to One. In between, it must pretend to connect, relate, be bound by cause and effect, be a friend here or an enemy there depending on clan or blood or social status. It is a necessary, natural drive in all of us: to belong. This question reveals a slightly elevated ego, as it originates in a kind of consciousness concerned with continuity – 'I want to change the world so that they remember me.'

One thinks the so-called 'you', or self, must be preserved forever, for it is the shadow-side of your soul, which is forever because its nature is timeless. We need to have some belonging, identity, and definition; then, with intelligence, one realises this is only a certain flavour of the total flow of the energy of life.

For ordinary people, the drive to serve and contribute to society helps form identity: 'I am of this race, this colour, this culture, this economic status,' and so on. Identity must be there. Without an identity and a well-defined profile, you will not transcend it to ever-present Reality, which is the energy of Life. This drive is a natural state.

The Giver is One

The giver or the server also benefits. We are all within the same stream of rising in intelligence to realise that ultimately there is a flow of energy in nature. So, the less there is this illusion of being separate as an 'I' who is helping others, the less there will be anxiety, sorrow, reproach, and regrets.

The giver is One. We are climbing the ladder of realising the origin is One; in-between the One appears as twos, and the conclusion and the destiny is One. To help others, the less you have expectations of reward, the more you will be rewarded, not in a visible but in a more subtle way – until such time as you find the giver is one, and the illusion or the shadow of me as the receiver is only to return me through intelligence back to the One.

It all comes down to connecting with stronger glues. There are thousands of different glues by virtue of which we connect. For instance, sharing a hobby or creative interest connects people. Sharing the same enemy can also connect us, which is the shadow of the ultimate glue: reverential, unconditional love. A most simple, but profound, glue is awareness of the air we breathe, for it may lead you to the inner meaning: we are all dependent on the same essence in every single moment. Ultimately, these glues connect me to awareness of my responsibilities as a steward on this earth, training to return to gatheredness beyond any glue.

Self-Reflection Questions

1. Consider why we are driven to contribute to society?
    - Examine the reasons why you are moved to serve or contribute to society.
2. Reflect upon durable and wholesome ways in which we can enhance the quality of a society?

Chapter Fifteen

Relationships

Would you talk about relationships - the possibilities and challenges that they pose in the development and the movement towards fulfilment?

Mirror Reflections

How can I have a good relationship if I am not properly related to my own soul? It is impossible. Everything is alien, everyone else is 'other', every minute is other, and all *others* are enemies because they do not connect with the real *One*. Relationships are always challenging, so I must start with the early realisation that contentment arises when my so-called ego, biography, profile, or personality is in unison with its source of energy. If that is not, then there is no true ground from which to relate.

Most relationships are often miserable because each person mirrors the other. I look in the mirror to put my hair right or make my face up, then I look in the mirror of the other until I realise that it is me. Most people in close relationships dislike the other, who really are just mirrors of their own behaviour. They dislike meanness because they are mean themselves, they dislike argumentativeness because they are argumentative. And so you begin to hate.

Instead of putting yourself right you throw a tantrum at the mirror. You complain 'You always put me down!', because the husband or the wife always want to appear as generous or good, but he or she sees their own shadow in the other.

Relationships are mirror reflections, which come down to your own adjustment of your own awareness. It is all about awareness. Be aware of the rise of this or that feeling. It is fine to feel negative emotions, but feel them and then change yourself, instead of blaming others.

Relationships and Unity

Everything we experience is within duality. So are relationships. The healthier a relationship, the more you just want to serve, without expectations. That means the relationship is reduced from duality and multiplicity to unity. You are only doing it for your own sake. So you lose the giver and the taker into the grace of oneness, that is all, until you find there are no 'others'.

You love your mother because essentially there is a love of the *rūh* within you. You love yourself. But through the love of the mother, you become more and more universal, until you discover through everywhere you look or hear or touch, there is only One, emerging as twos and threes and zillions.

Then you are prepared to gracefully, thankfully, leave your body and your mind behind to return, now with a certain measure of experience, back to that glorious zone of oneness without having the illusion that you can act. Or that you are free. Or that there is a you. You have done your job. Nature has done its job. That's it.

Self-Reflection Questions

1. How can you relate with anyone if you cannot relate to yourself?

2. Consider this in relation to the harmony of self and soul?

    - Comment on how one relationship helped you toward higher consciousness and how one hindered you.

Chapter Sixteen

Justice

What is Justice?

The Source of Justice

Justice is based on singularity. Once there is duality, there is a slight touch of injustice. Who is getting more and who is getting less? What is the difference between us and them? Take the example of identical twins raised in the same environment who, by the time they are in their teens, are distinct. How does that occur?

All these spirits have been exposed to the Cosmic Spirit. There is this wonderful allegory in the Qur'an. It says that all the spirits were exposed to the Lord of Spirits, and He said, 'Am I not your Lord?' They replied, 'Yes. Absolutely.' That is Oneness. That is the source of justice.

Once differentiation of identity begins then injustice begins, because now I am separate. Once the newly born baby begins to comprehend that there is space and time, that is the beginning of injustice. This reflects the growth of the ego, which is necessary. It must grow, in order to be demolished.

Humanity is One

Justice is Oneness, constant and eternal. Justice is that all souls, all spirits are the same. Justice is a cosmic, eternal truth. It can only be realised by the occurrence of a touch of injustice: I and It. I and them. I and other. That is the beginning of injustice.

We have made progress from tribal identity to a wider recognition that humanity is one and that everyone has human rights. But it is really the reverse. It is not about rights: it is about human responsibility and duty. Focussing on rights is quite basic. Yes, we do not want to kill anyone anymore, and perhaps we may even elect someone from a minority group to our cabinet and congratulate ourselves for embracing diversity. Yet this misses the crucial point, which is about what is in your own heart.

Can you really see others as souls, the same as you?

The Qur'an says that not until you see your enemy and regard him or her as your best friend will you be free from the prison of your identity. It may take a long time, it may take a brief time, it may just be the end of it. We do not know.

Self-Reflection Questions

1. 'Justice is sameness, Oneness, constant and eternal. Justice is that all souls, all spirits are the same.' Reflect upon this statement.

    - "Can you really see others as souls, the same as you?": Rate yourself on a scale of 1 to 10.

Chapter Seventeen

A Fulfilled Life

What does it Mean to Live a Fulfilled Life?

Calibration of Conditioned and Higher Consciousness

Living a so-called enlightened, or fulfilled, life means that your being has connected with higher consciousness, which is not definable. This calibration between your conditioned consciousness and higher consciousness reduces suffering. Your love of, and demands from, this constructed world are reduced, so your full being is less afflicted. This state reflects the combination of an earthly animal evolved over billions of years and a sacred cosmic light. That is all it means. A fulfilled life means you realise this is a transitory, temporary stage between the infinite unknown and the finite known, between self and soul.

One must be cognisant of the implication of using fashionable words and ideas regarding enlightenment, awakening and so on. The so-called awakened, fulfilled being, or the realised self, experiences less trauma, drama, and suffering in this world because they know beyond words that the experiences of this world are a construct of the mind. Our neuronal patterning returns repeatedly to the same ideas, always wanting security.

For thousands of years, the biggest drive in human life was justice, loyalty, duty, decency, and acceptability. Since the dawn of the new millennium, it is all changed. The commercialisation of life has left us with the illusion that the world owes us something. We behave and relate as if ecstatic well-being is something others can provide, so everybody falls into this illusion: 'Am I happy? Am I really happy? Do you think I am happy? I don't think I'm happy.' What is happiness really? Nobody seems to know.

Beyond Contentment

We ask, 'Am I content?', but how can you ever be content? The self is a shadow! How can a shadow be constant, still, and peaceful? Your real self is beyond contentment. You must discover that and be a soul. A good life was about duty, honesty, loyalty, sacrifice, but now it is all 'me, me, me!'

So we accumulate all sorts of useless waste: your cupboard is full of clothes and your stomach is full of rubbish and you end up in palliative care rather than witnessing perfection.

The purpose of life is Life itself. If you take all the other subsidiary things and make them the most important, then you have no life. You may have power, you may have money, but you know that you are not fulfilled. You are only fulfilled when you know that there is no definable, reliable entity called 'you'. It is only an outer encrustation of the Divine Presence, of Life itself.

Self-Reflection Questions

1. How do you understand and experience calibration with higher consciousness?

2. What does it mean to you to live a fulfilled life?

    - What actions can you take now that will facilitate leading a fulfilled life.

Postscript

Fulfilment implies permanent bliss and joyfulness and that can only occur if your consciousness of the Eternal is the basis of your state. This implies the loss of conditioned and lower consciousness. Lose your self and be at one with the soul.

AUTHOR'S BIOGRAPHY

SHAYKH FADHLALLA HAERI

Sufi, mystic and visionary, Shaykh Fadhlalla Haeri is an enlightened spiritual master. His life and works serve as a reminder that spirituality is a science and an art vitally relevant to our times.

Acknowledged as a master of self-knowledge and a spiritual philosopher, Shaykh Fadhlalla Haeri's role as a teacher grew naturally out of his own quest for self-fulfilment.

His informed awareness of the world around him compelled him to seek a truth that would reconcile the past with the present, the East with the West, the worldly with the spiritual. A link between the ancient wisdom teachings and our present time. He is a descendant of five generations of well-known and revered spiritual leaders, he has taught students throughout the world for over 40 years.

Selected Books by Shaykh Fadhlalla Haeri

Cosmology of the Self
Happiness in Life and After Death: An Islamic Sufi View
The Story of Creation in the Qur'an
Witnessing Perfection
Journey of the Self: A Sufi Guide to Personality
Decree and Destiny
The Essential Message of the Qur'an
ASK Course One: The Sufi Map of the Self
Spectrum of Reality
The Journey of the Universe as expounded in the Qur'an
Sufi Encounters: Sharing the Wisdom of the Enlightened Sufis

For more information on Shaykh Fadhlalla Haeri's books please visit www.zahrapublications.pub.

For more information on Shaykh Fadhlalla Haeri and his teachings please visit www.shaykhfadhlallahaeri.com and www.sfhfoundation.net

www.ingramcontent.com/pod-product-compliance
Lightning Source LLC
Chambersburg PA
CBHW060931180426
43192CB00045B/2890